For Jenny

Henry Holt and Company, Publishers since 1866
Henry Holt® is a registered trademark of Macmillan Publishing Group, LLC.
120 Broadway, New York, NY 10271 • mackids.com

Library of Congress Cataloging-in-Publication Data is available.

Our books may be purchased in bulk for promotional, educational, or business use. Please contact your local bookseller or the Macmillan Corporate and Premium Sales Department at(800) 221-7945 ext. 5442 or by email at MacmillanSpecialMarkets@macmillan.com.

First Edition, 2021
Book design by Cindy De la Cruz
Printed in China by RR Donnelley Asia Printing Solutions Ltd.,
Dongguan City, Guangdong Province.
Jeff Mack illustrated this book using Photoshop, ProCreate, custom digital brushes, cardboard, newsprint, and whatever else he could get away with.

ISBN 978-1-250-77715-7

1 3 5 7 9 10 8 6 4 2

Art is Everywhere

a book about Andy Warhol

by Jeff Mack

Henry Holt and Company
New York

Oh, hello.
I'm Andy.

This is the
story of my art.

I hope you like it.

Once upon a time, I drew shoes.

Lots of pretty shoes.
I drew them for a shoe company.

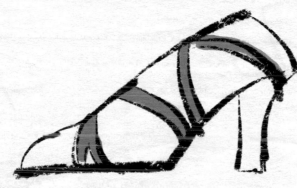

It was my job.

All day long, it was

shoe

shoe

shoe

shoe

shoe

shoe

shoe

shoe.

I felt like a robot in a factory. It was so cool.

Mom and I did everything together.
We lived together. We worked together.
We shopped for groceries together.
On Sunday, we went to church together.

This is me with my mom, Julia.
Doesn't she look like a real artist?

What does a real artist look like anyway?
When I was in art school,
I colored my hair bright green.

Did green hair make me an artist?
I don't think so.

I guess I just wanted
to be different.

After I moved to New York City,
I wore wigs. Lots of wigs.
My whole life long, it was

← Wig

Wig

Wig

Wig

Wig

Wig

Wig.

My hair was always changing.
But underneath it was still the
same me, over and over again.

I wanted my art to change with the times. So I drew the things I saw around me.

They're the same things we all see all day long.

Look. I drew this.
Isn't it pretty? It's soup.

Do you like soup?
We all like soup.

I drew lots of soup.

It looks just like the soup shelf at the grocery store.

So pretty.

Some people said my soup wasn't real art.
They said it was just soup.
I guess they didn't see soup
the same way I saw soup.
SOUP
SOUP
SOUP
SOUP
I think art is
about liking things.
It's about seeing the
things around us
in a new way.
Seeing them as pretty.

EVERYTHING is pretty. Don't you think?

Animals are pretty.

Cars are pretty.

Flowers are pretty.

Things you grow. Things you build. Things you buy.

Just look around you. ART is everywhere.

Look at her. Do you think SHE'S pretty?
She was a famous movie star.

I saw her face everywhere.
So I printed her over and over again.

Did I make her famous? Or did she make me famous?

And what about these boxes?
They're pretty, right?

Pretty cool.

I mean, gosh.
They're EXACTLY the same as the ones in the store.

I made them here in my factory.
Some people thought a machine made them.

But it was really me.

Look. I also made a movie.

It's the Empire State Building,
the most famous building in the world.

Isn't it pretty?

The lights. The clouds.
The city smog.

Do you like movies?

We all like movies.

My movie was eight hours long.

You could just sit and watch the Empire State Building

for eight hours.

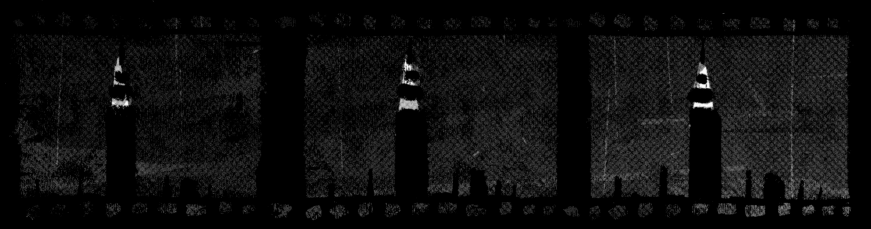

All night long.

Empire State Building, Empire State Building,

Empire State Building, Empire State Building,

Empire State Building, Empire State Building,

Empire State Building. It was very pretty.

Some people said it wasn't a real movie.

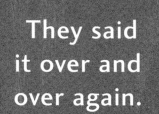

They said it over and over again.

The more they talked about it, the more famous my art became.

The more famous my art became, the more famous I became.

The more famous I became, the more people wanted to buy my art.

The more art they bought, the more art I made.

The more art I made, the more people said that it wasn't really art.

They said it over and over again. I got so confused.

How do you know when something is really art?

Or when it isn't?

Oh, look. These were my rock stars.
Don't they look cool? I think so.

Lou

Sterling

John

Nico

Moe

They played music at my factory parties.
Do you like music?

They played music while I showed my movies on them.

Movies and music and cow wallpaper and silver pillows floating like clouds.

It was all so pretty.

Look at this.

I made a magazine.

It's called *interVIEW*, and it's full of famous faces.

I saw these faces everywhere, over and over again.

What does it mean to be famous?

Soup is famous. Brillo boxes are famous.

The Empire State Building is famous.

If everyone were famous, who would really be famous?

I made a TV show too.

Everyone likes TV.
Right?

If you weren't famous, you could go on my TV show.

Then you would be a famous TV star.

One day, we'll all be stars.

TV stars.

Movie stars.

Rock stars.

All kinds of stars.

Do you like stars?

We all like stars.

One day, we will all be stars of our own shows,
and we will all like each other over and over again.
Gee . . . . Won't that be great?

Andy Warhol was an American artist who worked in New York City from 1949 to 1987. Like a mirror reflects everything you put in front of it, Andy wanted to reflect the time and place where he lived. So he used the mechanical tools of advertising, like photography and screen printing, to make pictures of the things he saw around him: newspapers, comic books, photos of movie stars, things you could buy in a supermarket. Even though he copied these images, his versions always looked like something only Andy Warhol could have made.

His kind of art became known as Pop art.

As time passed, Andy stretched his creativity by using newer and more popular types of media to share his ideas. He made rock records, films, magazines, and television programs. People around the world who had never visited an NYC art gallery before could now see him and his art on their television screens.

If he were alive today, what types of media do you think he'd be using to make his art? YouTube? Instagram? Snapchat? You know Andy. He liked everything.